The
Private
Life

THE 1975 LAMONT POETRY SELECTION
OF THE ACADEMY OF AMERICAN POETS

The Academy of American Poets made its first Lamont Poetry
Selection award in 1954. Since that time, the award has supported
the publication and distribution of twenty-one first books of poetry.
The 1975 Lamont Poetry Selection marks a change. This
distinguished award is now given to an American poet who has
already published one book in a standard edition and insures the
publication of that poet's second book of poems. Judges for 1975:
Alan Dugan, John Haines, Michael Harper.

The Private Life

 Poems by

LISEL MUELLER

LOUISIANA STATE

UNIVERSITY PRESS

Baton Rouge   1976

ISBN 0-8071-0182-6 (cloth)
ISBN 0-8071-0171-0 (paper)
Library of Congress Catalog Card Number 75-5350
Copyright © 1976 by Lisel Mueller
All rights reserved
Manufactured in the United States of America
Printed by Thomson-Shore, Dexter, Michigan
Designed by Albert Crochet

"A Nude by Edward Hopper," "On Reading an Anthology of Postwar German Poetry,"
"The Gift of Fire," "Life of a Queen," "Small Poem About the Hounds
and the Hares," "Historical Museum, Manitoulin Island," and "Sleepless"
appeared originally in *Poetry*.
"Reading the Brothers Grimm to Jenny" appeared originally in the *New Yorker*.
"A Farewell, a Welcome" appeared originally in the anthology *Inside Outer
Space: New Poems for the Space Age*, edited by Robert Vas Dias
(New York: Anchor Books, 1970).
"Messages" appeared originally in Volume I of *Voyages to the Inland Sea*
(La Crosse, Wisc.: Center for Contemporary Poetry, 1971).
"Snow," "Love Like Salt," "Palindrome," and "In Praise of Surfaces" appeared
originally in the chapbook *Life of a Queen* (La Crosse, Wisc.: Northeast/Juniper
Books, 1970).
Other poems originally appeared in *Shenandoah, Poetry Northwest, Cafe Solo, Sumac,
Arts in Society*, the Chicago *Tribune, Dunes House*, and *American Poetry Review*.

For Paul, still and again

Contents

I

We live in an occupied country, misunderstood;
justice will take us millions of intricate moves.
                                        —William Stafford

Whoever You Are: A Letter

Someone who does not know you
somewhere is cleaning his rifle,
carefully weighing the bullets
that will put you out of his life.

Someone, perhaps the figure
you see in the rearview mirror,
is living ahead to your death,
dreaming the sick world green.

Someone is already climbing
a tower in Texas, is halfway up,
is at the top, has sought you out
and lifts his gun as though this death
had anything to do with you.

Small Poem
About the Hounds and the Hares

After the kill, there is the feast.
And toward the end, when the dancing subsides
and the young have sneaked off somewhere,
the hounds, drunk on the blood of the hares,
begin to talk of how soft
were their pelts, how graceful their leaps,
how lovely their scared, gentle eyes.

Reading the Brothers Grimm
to Jenny

"Dead means somebody has to kiss you."

Jenny, your mind commands
kingdoms of black and white:
you shoulder the crow on your left,
the snowbird on your right;
for you the cinders part
and let the lentils through,
and noise falls into place
as screech or sweet roo-coo,
while in my own, real world
gray foxes and gray wolves
bargain eye to eye,
and the amazing dove
takes shelter under the wing
of the raven to keep dry.

Knowing that you must climb,
one day, the ancient tower
where disenchantment binds
the curls of innocence,
that you must live with power
and honor circumstance,
that choice is what comes true—
O, Jenny, pure in heart,
why do I lie to you?

Why do I read you tales
in which birds speak the truth
and pity cures the blind,
and beauty reaches deep
to prove a royal mind?
Death is a small mistake
there, where the kiss revives;
Jenny, we make just dreams
out of our unjust lives.

Still, when your truthful eyes,
your keen, attentive stare,
endow the vacuous slut
with royalty, when you match
her soul to her shimmering hair,

what can she do but rise
to your imagined throne?
And what can I, but see
beyond the world that is
when, faithful, you insist
I have the golden key—
and learn from you once more
the terror and the bliss,
the world as it might be?

The Gift of Fire

In memory of Norman Morrison, who burned himself to death
in front of the Pentagon on November 2, 1965

In a time of damnation
when the world needed a Savior,
when the dead gathered routinely,
comic-strip flat and blurred,

he took the god at his promise
and set himself on fire,
skin, brain, sex, smile

so we should see, really see
by that unbearable light
the flower of the single face,
the intricate moth of consciousness:

but he lived in the land of the one-eyed
where the blind is king.

Highway Poems

For Lucy and Jenny

> We keep coming back and coming back
> To the real: to the hotel instead of the hymns
> That fall upon it out of the wind
> —Wallace Stevens, "An Ordinary Evening in New Haven"

1

The narrow black veins on the map
will get you there, but the fat
red arteries get you there quicker
and without pain:
you can go from the head
to the toes of America
without seeing
a hospital or a jail,
without ever coming on tears
                    toys
                    wrinkles
                    scars
                    fists
                    guns
                    crossed fingers
                    broken teeth

2

Between the roof of the Howard Johnson
and the star of the Holiday Inn
falls the shadow
which is myself.

Question: am I real
when I exist only
inside a hot steel body
at 70 miles per hour
and when I'm freed, become
a certain car-door slam,
a brief pattern of footsteps
outside a numbered door?

3

Hardly anyone takes
the old state road anymore.
The town is dying,

its blood being pumped
into the new expressway
five miles east of here.
Sad and miraculous now,
transfigured by extinction,
are the ones who stay
to go down with the town:
the proprietor of the General Store
and the Restwell Cabins (vacancy always)
and the postmistress, his wife,
angel of government checks
and news from a world with receding walls.

4

Camping, you learn people
by their shoes in the toilet stalls.
The brown loafers support
white legs and a silver trailer;
the navy tennis shoes go
with Pepsodent and a black wig;
the tiny saddle shoes match a voice
that talks about being three;
and I must be a pair
of yellow sneakers, blue-patched at the toes,
although, being filled with my life,
I don't believe it.

5
Illinois, Indiana, Iowa
Austrian food is not served in Vienna,
and people in Paris drink Coke, not wine.
Lebanon has its Little League
and Warsaw its Civil War cannon.
Carthage is full of blondes,
and Cairo divides, American-style,
into white and black, money and rage.
Gnawbone keeps teasing, a tricky riddle,
and What Cheer defies punctuation,
but Stony Lonesome is all that it says.
I have seen Hindustan—Hoosier twang,
no belly dancing allowed—
and I have been in Arcadia:

one street by a railroad track,
blue chicory, goldenrod.

O telltale country, fact and mirage,
coat of many colors
stitched in homesickness, threaded with dreams,
land of the seven fat cows,
is it finished, your poem?

6

We keep coming back to the old hotel,
to the old Main Street, in the old part of town,
to the tottering giant, the elephant
sagging on concrete feet.

We keep coming back to the white-railed porch,
the geraniums and the wicker chairs,
the glass doors and the Persian carpet,
the banquet hall with the chandeliers
where the Chamber of Commerce meets and talks
about pride and achievement, while the stores
on the block are vacant, their windows blind,
their clerks gone to the big new mall
outside of town, where the chain stores are
with check-out lanes and shopping carts,
where shoplifting is a crime.

We keep coming back to the corpses of elms,
imagining shade, umbrellas of peace,
imagining grandparents, newspapers, cups,
people out walking, the ticket booth
of the movie theater occupied—
were times really better when the hotel
served the best Sunday dinner around
and the bridal suite was booked solid,
when the governor campaigned on the steps,
promising dollars for votes?

We keep coming back to what we gave up;
remember, we never wanted to live here
in the days of parades and the Firemen's Ball
and the high school musical once a year.
No, these are deathbed visits: regrets,

surprising grief and sudden love,
terror of loss, the need to lay
hands on the past before it is gone;
hold on to the knowledge at least, if not
the stairs and walls of our history;
walk away weeping at least, assured
that sometime, a long time ago,
we came from somewhere, that we are real.

The Fall of the Muse

Her wings are sold for scrap,
her tiara goes to the museum.
She takes off her purple gown,
her long gloves.
In her underwear she is anyone.

Even when she is naked, they laugh.
It's not enough, they shout.
Take off your pubic hair,
mutilate your breasts,
cut off a finger,
put a patch on your left eye.

Now she is one of us.
She laughs the small laugh of the ordinary.
She gives us all equal kisses.
She counts her money at inaugural balls.
She is searched at airports.
She depends on sleeping pills.
She betrays art with life.
She lectures on the catharsis of drivel.
She learns about Mount Olympus from quiz shows.

She moves in a circle of victims;
they make her eat her heart in public.
She has been bled so many times
her blood has lost its color.
She comes on the stage on all fours
but insists that her teeth be straightened.

Democratic, she sits with us.
We share the flat bread of affluence,
the suicidal water;
we kill each other with jokes.
She wears false eyelashes
when she throws herself off the bridge.

The Biographer

A biography is something one invents.
                    —Louis-Ferdinand Céline

God knows I've used
what surgical skills I have
to open you up through minor incisions
—larger ones might not have healed,
left you a cripple or a corpse,
and I love you too much for that.

For years, I lived
on a diet of your words,
letters, diaries, the collected works,
till they dropped from my mouth like pits
each time I spoke, and my friends
could smell you on my breath.

I took the journeys you took,
walked in your tracks like a Chinese wife;
asleep, I spoke in your dreams.
I would have eaten your heart;
like Snow White's mother I wanted to turn into you,
but chaste and tricky, you slipped through your facts.

I came to live in your house,
restored your pictures, bought back your books,
discovered the key to your desk,
moved the yellow chair to the window
—and now you come in, asking
whose house this is.

January Afternoon,
with Billie Holiday
For Studs Terkel

Her voice shifts as if it were light,
from chalk to parchment to oil.
I think of the sun this morning,
how many knives were flashed
through black, compliant trees;
now she has aged it with her singing,
turned it to milk thinned with water,
a poor people's sun, enough
knowledge to go around.

I want to dance, to bend
as gradually as a flower,
release a ball in slow motion
to follow in the marvelous path
of an unfolding jet streak,
love's expansive finger
across the cheek of the sky,
"Heaven, I'm in heaven . . ."

The foolish old songs were right,
the heart does, actually, ache
from trying to push beyond
itself, this room, the world,
all that can be imagined;
space is not enough space
for its sudden immensity

I am not what you think
This is not what I wanted

Desire has no object, it simply happens,
rises and floats, lighter than air—
but she knows that. Her voice scrapes
against the innocent words of the song;
tomorrow is something she remembers.

Life of a Queen

1. Childhood

For two days her lineage is in doubt,
then someone deciphers the secret message.
They build a pendulous chamber
for her, and stuff her with sweets.

Workers keep bringing her royal jelly.
She knows nothing of other lives,
about digging in purple crocus
and round dances in the sun.

Poor and frail little rich girl,
she grows immense in her hothouse.
Whenever she tries to stop eating,
they open her mouth and force it down.

2. The Flight

She marries him in midair;
    for a moment
he is ennobled, a prince.

She gives the signal
    for their embrace;
over too soon. O, nevermore.

Bruised, she drags herself from
    his dead body,
finds her way back exhausted.

She is bathed, curtains are drawn.
    Ten thousand lives
settle inside her belly.

Now to the only labor she knows.
    She remembers
nothing of him, or their fall.

3. The Recluse

They make it plain
her term is over.
No one comes;
they let her starve.

The masses, her children,
whip up sweets
for a young beauty
who is getting fat.

Nothing to do.
Her ovaries paper,
her sperm sac dust,
she shrivels away.

A crew disassembles
her royal cell.
Outside, a nation
crowns its queen.

Historical Museum,
Manitoulin Island

After a while it dawns on us
we are intruders, in spite of the sign
and the box for donations. The knitted white
stockings, limp from too many washings,
droop before us like worn-out tongues
and still insist on their owner
(feet that wore them, hands that darned them),
her name and her yellow picture
—yes, but not yellow enough
that we should finger such secret parts.

We touch Mrs. Thompson's long cotton nightgown
and discover we are touching babies,
those that survived, and the two
in the graveyard beyond the wall.
We see that the golden snuffbox
and the doll with human hair
are dreams locked behind glass,
and when we come to the hard-eyed
tintype of Mr. and Mrs. Lewis
above their big double bed
and find beside it "Lucy Grey"
copied in violet ink,
we have forced another secret.

We're opening lives like lockets,
rummaging through possessions
stripped from still warm bodies.
Silence accuses us, level-eyed
like the poor who did not know they were poor,
the brave who did not know they were brave,
the enduring who endure in this room.

They had no right to call this a museum.
Not yet. We thank the lady
with tinted hair by the door
and reenter our summery lives,
the ones they gave us: easy love,
warm rooms, soft speech, long years.

17

Spell for a Traveler

From the harbor of sleep bring me the milk of childhood,
from the ocean of silence bring me a grain of salt,
from the city of chances bring me my lucky number,
from the lookout of morning bring me a speckled egg,
from the palace of mirrors send me my old, lost self,
from the hill of bones send me a drop of your blood.

From the province of spring everlasting
bring back a rose that remains half-open,
from the drydock of mute old men
bring back the miracle of a tear,
from the delta of good intentions
bring back the seed that will change a life.

From the fields of the dispossessed bring me a donkey
with Byzantine eyes, from the wells of the mad
bring me the bell and lantern of heaven.

From the bay of forgetfulness come back with my name,
from the cave of despair come to me empty-handed,
from the strait of narrow escapes come back, come back.

II

We humanize what is going on in the world and in ourselves only by speaking of it, and in the course of speaking of it we learn to be human.
　　　　　　　　　　　　　　—Hannah Arendt

Alive Together

Speaking of marvels, I am alive
together with you, when I might have been
alive with anyone under the sun,
when I might have been Abélard's woman
or the whore of a Renaissance pope
or a peasant wife with not enough food
and not enough love, with my children
dead of the plague. I might have slept
in an alcove next to the man
with the golden nose, who poked it
into the business of stars,
or sewn a starry flag
for a general with wooden teeth.
I might have been the exemplary Pocahontas
or a woman without a name
weeping in Master's bed
for my husband, exchanged for a mule,
my daughter, lost in a drunken bet.
I might have been stretched on a totem pole
to appease a vindictive god
or left, a useless girl-child,
to die on a cliff. I like to think
I might have been Mary Shelley
in love with a wrong-headed angel,
or Mary's friend. I might have been you.
This poem is endless, the odds against us are endless,
our chances of being alive together
statistically nonexistent;
still we have made it, alive in a time
when rationalists in square hats
and hatless Jehovah's Witnesses
agree it is almost over,
alive with our lively children
who—but for endless ifs—
might have missed out on being alive
together with marvels and follies
and longings and lies and wishes
and error and humor and mercy
and journeys and voices and faces
and colors and summers and mornings
and knowledge and tears and chance.

My Grandmother's Gold Pin

The first fleur-de-lis is for green-stemmed glasses with swirls, which were called Romans / for the cow with the brown fleece, which said moo when we bent its neck / for the elegant braids on my grandfather's shabby jacket; my grandfather, who was poor and proud and loving:

The second is for the upright on which my aunt played Schubert Impromptus (though we shivered with joy at "Rustles of Spring") / for the cactus which bumped the ceiling / for the silk and ebony fans that clicked into bloom in my grandmother's cold bedroom / for the same dark dress she wore every day, making her bosom cozy under her round smile / for snowdrops with modestly lowered heads, which we bought at the corner for every one of her birthdays, rushing spring by two days:

The third is for cherry soup, beer soup and chocolate soup, served in thin china bowls with gold edges / for my grandfather's walking stick with its silver head swinging, when we walked past red rhododendrons and ponds full of hand-fed swans / for the hours of pachisi / for red, lustrous dominoes, heavy as gems in the hand / for the card tricks up my grandfather's sleeve; merry secrets of one who was totally deaf, who was gentle and gay and a child among children:

The fourth is for a white china hen with fresh eggs in her belly / for darning days, when my grandmother traded us mended socks for crisp brown flounder / for my grandfather's treasure of butterflies / for Roman candles, his credible galaxies / for the red leather albums of postage stamps, precious untouchables which went, one by one, for the roof over their heads:

And the pearl in the center is for remembrance / for never forgetting the war, flight, madness and hunger which killed them / for never forgiving that death in an animal shed / for the flowers I'd bring, if I could, to the grave on the other side of a Wall which should be a metaphor or a bad dream / and for the passion of sorrow, senseless and pure, which is all I can give in return to them, who were truly good:

And that, my daughter, is why I wear it / and because it is all I have left of an age when people believed the heart was an organ of goodness, and light was stronger than darkness,

that death came to you in your proper time:
An age when the dream of Man nearly came true.

On Reading an Anthology of
Postwar German Poetry

What times are these, when
it is almost a crime to talk about trees
because that means being silent about so much evil?
                    —Bertolt Brecht

America saved me
and history played me false:
I was not crushed
under rubble, nor was I beaten
along a frozen highway;
my children are not dead
of postwar hunger;
my love is back with his brain
intact, his toes accounted for;
I have coaxed no one
into the chamber of death.

My habits have not been broken.
For me, rock stands
for dignity, fire
is an element, the moon
is not necessarily poisoned,
snow exists for its own sake.

I know enough to refuse to say
that life is good,
but I act as though it were.
And skeptical about love, I survive
by the witness of my own.

I am, among these poets,
a Briar Rose, a Rip Van Winkle,
a stranger to the beginnings
they make from the stench of evil,
the burial of Man:
I marvel, as The Word
rises from bedrock, lifts,
and splits, a living cell,
into its destinies.

Untitled

Yes, we were happy that Sunday, walking
through mild blue patches of phlox
and dark red wake-robin stands
along the creek. Don't ask me what
switch in my mind flashed on,
unbidden, the Algerian girl
who had a bottle jammed into her
to make her talk:

                I did not know
she was still there, my antilife,
with her dark red wound.

Report to the National
Commission on Violence

In the beginning it was my life
against the life of my brothers and sisters.
The murder took place in the dark, in the sea;
winner take all was the only rule.

Later, I tried to kill
my mother, jailer who held me captive
nine months in her tight black cell.
She nursed and forgave me, said
she could not remember the wound, the pain.

Then came the night of the frog,
the lovesick beast that croaked
its way to my plate, my bed.
I smashed it against the wall
to free the man, the prince
under the damp disguise:
together we burned the animal skin.

There was the night when the squatter
inside my body broke out
with knife and saw and hammer.
After the struggle, we lay exhausted,
she on my breast, I with my arms around her,
the daughter that fed on my marrow-bone.

Things have been quieter lately. Only
a child's occasional terror splits open the night,
and every June of his life the dog sniffs out
a nest of young rabbits and breaks their necks.
Each June of my life I learn to forgive him.

Two Poems Written in the Age of the Great Migrations

1. Moving Day

Blow down the house of bricks,
there is another, bigger,
two thousand miles down the road.
Pull up the roots, they are shallow yet,
in another year they might shriek.

If bones start to sing
under the freeway,
marvelous songs of your cast-off life,
look straight ahead, outrace them;
lament over loss itself is lost
at the speed of sameness.

Send the heavy possessions ahead.
Haul the packable souls of children.
What can't be carted or burned or sold
must stay behind (*O nondisposable love,*
if I turn once more, I'll grieve myself into salt).

At regular intervals, golden arches,
rainbows designed to bridge
the snap of dislocation:
Lethe was never so well engineered
to exhaust the old dog of memory
which tags along for a while,

and after the next junction
you will give up throwing
crumbs over your shoulder
to mark the way back home.

2. The Same, in Spanish

Down comes the neon of the poor,
the row of starry diapers;
the wind has slipped
a letter under the door
postmarked *Esperanza*.

Again
the rugs are folded,
the dishes put in the cardboard box.
The mattresses stay on the floor.

The table belongs to the landlord.
The TV is broken anyway.

The children jump
on the Green Stamp suitcase;
they have run out of fingers
for counting schools.

Pray that the car starts.

Country Road: Illinois

Look at this landscape,
those shapeless multiple greens,
haphazard, inhumanly lost:
but for the barns,
the colorful mothers,
settling them all like wayward children
around their sturdy skirts,

where would all that loneliness go?

Amazing Grace

State and Madison, Chicago

Blind, black and believing
—archaic trinity—
he fixes burned-out eyes
on an abandoned heaven
as he shouts and chants
his hoarse, relentless gospel:
PUT GOD BACK IN YOUR LIVES.

Whose god, old man? What you hear
are sounds of summer and money,
as unbelieving waves
spill past you every time
the stoplight clicks to green;
whose god, in what disguise?
We carry our gods in our skins,
our wallets, our sons and daughters;
for some of us, angels
stream from the jab of a needle,
for others, infinite mercy
listens beside a couch;
we pray
to the promise of stars and numbers
if we are lonely,
and if we are young, to the smile
that curls in the lotus of flesh;
we pick and choose from among
patented miracles—
shall we be saved by a shiny pill
or a shining vision?

*Once I was blind, but now
I see*, he shouts at us,
at the polluted sky.
His face is rapt, his eyes
are two locked doors.

Messages

May, 1970

Outside the window, messages pile up,
congratulations, valentines,
spring bouquets with assurances
about the dancing feet of the dead
which we swore we had had enough of.

A day of glorious weather
is all it takes to corrupt us;
we betray the grief we wanted to keep
like a broken watch, we decide
the anger we thought was integrity
was, after all, only anger.

We fill the mouths of the speechless
with tongues and delight in their news,
forgetting who put it there;
we receive like the woman whose teeth
contain too much metal, who eavesdrops
on the radio signals of fishermen
and lies awake on her coil of springs
listening to music from God knows where.

After the shootings, we understood
the stiffened air, the reversal
of tulips from silk to paper
and knew why the ground resisted
the small weaponry of our heels.

We breathe all things into speech;
we listen, we respond.
The doorknob insists that we turn it,
an unopened letter demands its rights,
dogs talk to us with their bodies
and accept our answer in words.
Holes ask for rain, the stunted corpse of an elm
is revealed as a sign. We keep breaking
the code of the dead, we reply.

What the Dog Perhaps Hears

If an inaudible whistle
blown between our lips
can send him home to us,
then silence is perhaps
the sound of spiders breathing
and roots mining the earth;
it may be asparagus heaving,
headfirst, into the light
and the long brown sound
of cracked cups, when it happens.
We would like to ask the dog
if there is a continuous whirr
because the child in the house
keeps growing, if the snake
really stretches full length
without a click and the sun
breaks through clouds without
a decibel of effort;
whether in autumn, when the trees
dry up their wells, there isn't a shudder
too high for us to hear.

What is it like up there
above the shut-off level
of our simple ears?
For us there was no birth-cry,
the newborn bird is suddenly here,
the egg broken, the nest alive,
and we heard nothing when the world changed.

Monarchs

It was always their season, they
were always crossing mountains
and waters and borders, emerging
from special trains to get to each other,
visit in spas, review troops,
attend coronations, arrange alignments
and marry. They carried jewels and genes
between Copenhagen and Windsor Castle,
Darmstadt, St. Petersburg, Berlin,
object lessons in why
cousins should not marry
—"think of the czarevitch
bleeding to death, except
for a crazy monk's black magic"—
turning to one another
as if they could mate with no one else,
a species, distinct, dying out.

Their winged namesakes gather
on the republican beaches
of North America in September,
their orange and black coats of arms
a magnificent show in the crackling sun,
their sensitive double scepters
greeting each other as kin,
fellow aristocrats whom the birds
won't touch. They follow the flow of water
south, in slow motion, a fleet
of delicate nobles heading
for the palace of Montezuma,
patriarch of the orange-skinned.
They survive the difficult journey
intact, triumphant. But the return
is against the wind, a flight
into hostile country. It is time
to give up privilege, become
prolific like the poor,
who bank on the waste of numbers
to insure one single life,

time to deposit a mass of eggs
on the nearest milkweed

and die into the air,
traceless, without the trappings
of final rites and tears.

Palindrome

There is less difficulty—indeed, no logical difficulty
at all—in imagining two portions of the universe, say
two galaxies, in which time goes one way in one galaxy and
the opposite way in the other. . . . Intelligent beings in each galaxy
would regard their own time as "forward" and time in the other
galaxy as "backward."
                    —Martin Gardner in *Scientific American*

Somewhere now she takes off the dress I am
putting on. It is evening in the antiworld
where she lives. She is forty-five years away
from her death, the hole which spit her out
into pain, impossible at first, later easing,
going, gone. She has unlearned much by now.
Her skin is firming, her memory sharpens,
her hair has grown glossy. She sees without glasses,
she falls in love easily. Her husband has lost his
shuffle, they laugh together. Their money shrinks,
but their ardor increases. Soon her second child
will be young enough to fight its way into her
body and change its life to monkey to frog to
tadpole to cluster of cells to tiny island to
nothing. She is making a list:
             Things I will need in the past
                  lipstick
                  shampoo
                  transistor radio
                  Alice Cooper
                  acne cream
                  5-year diary with a lock
She is eager, having heard about adolescent love
and the freedom of children. She wants to read
Crime and Punishment and ride on a roller coaster
without getting sick. I think of her as she will
be at fifteen, awkward, too serious. In the
mirror I see she uses her left hand to write,
her other to open a jar. By now our lives should
have crossed. Somewhere sometime we must have
passed one another like going and coming trains,
with both of us looking the other way.

Leveling with Each Other

It hurts to pull off the old
disguises and patches. They stick,
the shields, veils, pasties,
the band-aids of aquiescence,
the diaphragm over the soul.

How to scrape away
centuries of makeup
to get to the grain of ourselves
after being born
pretending not to see
through one another, pretending
to see what men have seen?
Con artists, in too deep
to call each other's bluff.

Midnight: time to unmask.
In Viennese operettas
maids become mistresses and vice versa,
in fairy tales the glamorous stranger
becomes a household drudge.
Here in America we reveal
our lives like strippers, bit by bit,
small scar by minor wrinkle,
before an audience of our peers

until one of us lets fly
and dazzles us all with her nakedness,
her glorious black and blue.

A Voice in the Dark

A river within the cave has spawned fish with
no eyes because of the eternal darkness.
                    —From a pamphlet about Mammoth Cave

When we stop having children
our breasts fall,
the oil wells under our skin dry up

Waistlines are left to our daughters,
our legs appear in butcher shops

We are neutered, like cats,
only more slowly

Hair and teeth become relics
as useless as tonsils

It is assumed we adapt
to being invisible
except under infrared light

But we continue to put our arms
around our lives as always

We haggle to get our share of the world
at the old bargain price

We tolerate our mirrors,
they tell us nothing about ourselves

Sleepless

No use pushing against the dark,
the tomb is shut.
No one hears my pounding,
they have gone away forever.

By mistake I was laid out
along with the others,
the peaceful dead.
I am the only one left alive.

The man beside me is still warm,
but the switch of memory is broken.
For a long time
he made his home in my body;
now he will never know
I alone was not taken
when life on the planet became extinct.

When the birds jump the deadline
of dawn, I do not believe them.
Only later, when
the gray gauze flag
goes up against my window,
do I know I have been saved.
                    Weightless at last,
I float out of my skin:
sleepers, blessed spirits,
wait for me.

Snow

Telephone poles relax their spines;
sidewalks go under. The nightly groans
of aging porches are put to sleep.
Mercy sponges the lips of stairs.

While we talk in the old concepts
—time that was, and things that are—
snow has leveled the stumps of the past
and the earth has a new language.

It is like the scene in which the girl
moves toward the hero
who has not yet said, "Come here."

Come here, then. Every ditch
has been exalted. We are covered with stars.
Feel how light they are, our lives.

 III

A wish, come true, is life.

—Randall Jarrell

The Private Life

What happens, happens in silence:

The man from New York City
feels himself going insane
and flies to Brazil to rest,

The piano student in Indiana
lovingly gathers the prune pits
Horowitz left on his plate
the only time he ate breakfast there,

My daughter daydreams of marriage,
she has suddenly grown
three inches taller than I,

And now, this icy morning,
we find another tree,
an aspen, doubled over,
split in two at the waist:
no message, no suicide note.

*　　*　　*

Fruit market:
age-spotted avocados,
lemons with goose flesh;
navel oranges,
pears with flushed cheeks;
apples like buttocks,
pineapples like stockades,
coconut heads with instructions:
"Pierce the eyes with an awl,
allowing the milk to run out,
then tap hard with a hammer
until the outer covering cracks—"

life, our violent history,
lies speechless and mild in these bins.

*　　*　　*

We are being eaten by words.
My face is smeared with headlines.
My lungs, blue tubes, are always on.
You come home smelling of printer's ink.

The teletype is a dragon's mouth;
ripped out, its tongue grows back
at the speed of sound:

5,000 tons of explosives were dropped
The terrorist wore a business suit
His late model Triumph was found overturned
She said she had taken fertility drugs
The boy stood on the burning deck
The girl's body was found in a cornfield
The President joked with newsmen
The two youths were killed execution-style
The National Safety Council reported
A spokesman for the hospital said
The blond actress disclosed

YOUR HOUSE IS ON FIRE, YOUR CHILDREN ARE GONE

Stop it. What happens,
happens in silence:
in a red blood cell,
a curl in the brain,
in the ignorant ovum,
the switched-on nerves;

it happens in eyes before the scream,
in memory when it boils over,
in the ravine of conscience,
in the smile that says, *Come to bed.*

Today—my snow-capped birthday—
our red hibiscus is blooming again.
Months of refusal; now
one sudden silent flower,
one inscrutable life.

On a Photograph of
Randall Jarrell

Thick beard, ruled forehead, laugh lines
above high cheekbones, slender wrists and hands
writing; this much of you I see. Also
a strip of wall and curtain. The rest
I imagine: Elektra's obsessed voice
on the phonograph, a sketch of the Brothers Grimm,
Rilke's *New Poems* with notes in the margins,
visits from children, your girls—always girls,
for gentleness was your style and your reprieve
from Hansel and Gretel's forest, which must be
just outside. Girls and survivors,
and bats, whose slandered faces you redeemed
from our disgust. Bats love their babies too.
O waker of true princesses, I love you.

              *   *   *   *

A death has come
between the lines of this poem.
I look at you differently now,
discover the downward slant of your eyes,
the long-practiced patience which shows in the way
you hold your arms. Elektra is singing
unbearable music, her ecstasy blooms like a wound
now her brother is dead. What are we except
killers and sufferers? Still, you quietly walked
into your death one night in North Carolina.
A wish, come true, is life, you said. Having had your wish,
you blew out the birthday candles all at once.

The Late News

For months, numbness
in the face of broadcasts;
I stick to my resolution
not to bleed
when my blood helps no one.

For months, I accept
my smooth skin,
my gratuitous life as my due;
then suddenly, a crack—
the truth seeps through like acid,
a child without eyes to weep with
weeps for me, and I bleed
as if I were still human.

Divorce

We never saw her except
flat against the big trunk.

Now that it's cut away
we see she has
branches, leaves, tiny blossoms.

There are new shoots
and, on old leaves, white blotches.
Tart red berries grow from the shock
of living out in the open.

A Nude by Edward Hopper
For Margaret Gaul

The light
drains me of what I might be,
a man's dream
of heat and softness;
or a painter's
—breasts cozy pigeons,
arms gently curved
by a temperate noon.

I am
blue veins, a scar,
a patch of lavender cells,
used thighs and shoulders;
my calves
are as scant as my cheeks,
my hips won't plump
small, shimmering pillows:

but this body
is home, my childhood
is buried here, my sleep
rises and sets inside,
desire
crested and wore itself thin
between these bones—
I live here.

In Praise of Surfaces

1

When I touch you
with hands or mouth,
I bless your skin,
the sweet rind
through which you breathe,
the only part
I can possess. Even
that branch of you
which moves inside me
does not deliver your soul:
one flesh is all
the mystery we were promised.

2

To learn about the invisible,
look at the visible, says
the Talmud. I have seen you
for so long you are
ground into the walls,
so long I can't remember
your face when you're away,
so long I have to look
each night when you come home
at the tall surprise you bring
me, time and time again.

3

Words too are surfaces
scraped or shaken loose.
When I listen to you
I pick up rocks,
shells, algae
brought up from darkness.
Sometimes I
come close to catching
a fish bare-handed;
angling, I always fail.
No skin diver, I
could never reach bottom;
rock by wet rock,
piecemeal,
I collect you.

Seven

1

I cannot remember the first room
except in a dream
in which
I am a fish
thrown up on land,
fighting the hooks of the sun,
gasping,
            all mouth.

2

The second room kept expanding,
I could not keep up with its walls.

I licked the compound of salt and snow
from a gleaming spoon. I touched lives
of wool and glass. The unspeakable name
of the future hummed in my milky breath.

Space-child, I discovered freedom,
        billions of disorderly stars.

3

In the third room children
were playing the game
of good and evil.

"Choose," they said, extending
identical silver coins.

I looked at them for a clue
but they only
stared, like offended gods.

4

The door to the fourth room stuck;
they were trying to keep me out.
They were showing
a slide of a naked girl
cradling a fox. Its paw
lay on her breast, but its eyes,
its mandarin eyes, were on me.

"Can a fox smile?" I asked.
            They turned

and I saw I was naked.

5

The fifth room was totally empty;
all the walls were glass.

Birds kept crashing into the panes.
They hit the pavement, their breaking eyes
open, too lonely to be afraid.

6

I entered the sixth room blindfold;
they turned me around, once, twice.
"Remember, you must follow
the first one you touch . . ."
        I reached,
somehow I knew where you were.

7

I cannot open the last door,
none of the keys fit.

Yes, I have been warned,
have heard the rumors,

but have heard also
of a place as still as animal eyes,
as private as the explosions
inside a child's bones

and I will wait here
for the watchman
with his belt of keys.

Colorado

1. Specimen Mountain

We wheeze like asthmatics, halfway up.
The children ask the sensible question,
knowing there is no sensible answer.
They feel it too, whatever it is
in us that insists, *possess, possess,*
scratch your initials, touch the snow,
take a photograph, plant a flag,
steal a crumb of the summit.
We stuff our pockets with relics,
splinters of lava rock,
brown dried-up mountain blood,
and start again, toward cold, toward light,
for no other reason than that it is there.

2. The Drive

The highway cuts mountains in half.
Thanks to a conqueror's genius
we drive on this marvelous road,
civilizing the mountains,
turning stone into flesh.

Turning stone into flesh,
I look at an old man's hand,
discover a lopped-off finger
pointing to clouds, an arm
wedged between crooked teeth.

Profiles appear down the road,
shoulders, knees, a dog,
a loaf of bread on a shelf.
I stare the wilderness down
and put a wart on its nose.

Eaves and sills and chairs—
what I see is a sort of home,
a place one could get used to.
Already I call them ours,
this furniture, these walls.

3. Above the Tree Line

Who would have thought we could drive
straight up into the air
and arrive in Alaska, that we could have
the Arctic in Colorado!
Survival country: here
we can't see the sedum and saxifrage
unless we get down on all fours,
nor decipher the Arctic gentian,
how it lies low to the killer wind.
We learn to see slowly; our eyes
have to get used to the minimal
as they do to the dark. Then the miracles
come almost too fast: the glitter
of mica, lichen the color of pumpkin,
lichen the color of young spring peas
jump from the gray. A speckled rock
walks and turns into a ptarmigan,
stands still and turns into rock.
Inside a granite crevice
a population too dense
to be numbered, thrives in peace.
Out of the wind, our children
throw off their jackets, disappear
and pelt us from some hiding place.

Naming the Animals

Until he named the horse
                    horse,
hoofs left no print on the earth,
manes had not been invented,
swiftness and grace were not married.

Until he named the cow
                    cow,
no one slept standing up,
no one saw through opaque eyes,
food was chewed only once.

Only after he named the fish
                    fish,
did the light put on skins
of yellow and silver oil,
revealing itself as a dancer
and high-jump champion of the world,

just as later
he had to name the woman
                    love
before he could put on the knowledge
of who she was, with her small hands.

Love Like Salt

It lies in our hands in crystals
too intricate to decipher

It goes into the skillet
without being given a thought

It spills on the floor, so fine
we step all over it

We carry a pinch behind each eyeball

It breaks out on our foreheads

We store it inside our bodies
in secret wineskins

At supper, we pass it around the table
talking of holidays by the sea

The Concert

In memory of Dimitri Mitropoulos

The harpist believes there is music
in the skeletons of fish

The French horn player believes
in enormous golden snails

The piano believes in nothing
and grins from ear to ear

Strings are scratching their bellies
openly, enjoying it

Flutes and oboes complain
in dialects of the same tongue

Drumsticks rattle a calfskin
from the sleep of another life

because the supernatural crow
on the podium flaps his wings

and death is no excuse

A Real Toad in a Real Garden

Each spring
after the big rains
we find a toad at our doorstep,
a small night visitor,
calm and squat, like Buddha.

If he is a god, he takes
trouble disguising himself.
Neither swan nor bull,
he has no chance with women
in his no-color body
of warts, with eyes that pop
like oversized map tacks,
a drab thing, unassuming
as a hunched, wet leaf
left on the ground all winter.

But who knows? Blessings
come in strange shapes and sizes,
and in old tales
the kindest magic
is locked in the least of bodies.

Who knows, when we come home
from an evening in the city
to the damp smells of earth
and the clear tracks
of the Dipper over our roof,
what household spirit we scare away,
what patron of marriage, what
supernatural sponsor
of healthy children and natural death,

whose great leap this is?

Burned Out

Freedom's just another word for nothin' left to lose.
—Kris Kristofferson

Oppressed by bedspreads
maneuvered by knobs
shadowed by mailmen
shackled by keys
possessed by engines
subdued by pills
strangled by schedules
assaulted by words
subverted by money
broken by shoes—
all those years
how we longed to be free!

I'm here to help you
said Brother Fire
(rash Brother Fire
quick to oblige)—
stripped off the bedspreads
ripped out the knobs
smoked out the mailmen
blasted the keys
blew up the engines
knocked down the pills
chewed up the schedules
swallowed the words
stole all the money
danced on the shoes—
handed us freedom
nothing to lose

Neighbors came running
arms full of mercy
waved flowered bedspreads
screwed on the knobs
tracked down the mailmen
made shiny keys
spurred us with engines
nursed us with pills
braced us with schedules

fed us soft words
healed us with money
received us with shoes—
and we said *Bless you
sweet life, welcome back*

A Farewell, a Welcome

After the lunar landings

Good-bye pale cold inconstant
tease, you never existed
therefore we had to invent you

    Good-bye crooked little man
    huntress who sleeps alone
    dear pastor, shepherd of stars
    who tucked us in Good-bye

Good riddance phony prop
con man moon
who tap-danced with June
to the tender surrender
of love from above

Good-bye decanter of magic liquids
fortuneteller *par excellence*
seducer incubus medicine man
exile's sanity love's sealed lips
womb that nourished the monstrous child
and the sweet ripe grain Good-bye

    We trade you in as we traded
    the evil eye for the virus
    the rosy seat of affections
    for the indispensable pump
we say good-bye as we said good-bye
to angels in nightgowns to Grandfather God

Good-bye forever Edam and Gorgonzola
cantaloupe in the sky
night watchman, one-eyed loner
wolves nevertheless
are programed to howl Good-bye
    forbidden lover good-bye
    sleepwalkers will wander
    with outstretched arms for no reason
    while you continue routinely
    to husband the sea, prevail
    in the fix of infant strabismus
Goodbye ripe ovum women will spill their blood

in spite of you now lunatics wave good-bye
accepting despair by another name

Welcome new world to the brave old words
Peace Hope Justice
Truth Everlasting welcome
ash-colored playground of children
happy in airy bags
never to touch is never to miss it

Scarface hello we've got you covered
welcome untouchable outlaw
with an alias in every country
salvos and roses you are home
our footprints stamp you mortal

Hope

It hovers in dark corners
before the lights are turned on,
   it shakes sleep from its eyes
   and drops from mushroom gills,
     it explodes in the starry heads
     of dandelions turned sages,
        it sticks to the wings of green angels
        that sail from the tops of maples.

It sprouts in each occluded eye
of the many-eyed potato,
   it lives in each earthworm segment,
   surviving cruelty,
     it is the motion that runs
     from the eyes to the tail of a dog,
        it is the mouth that inflates the lungs
        of the child that has just been born.

It is the singular gift
we cannot destroy in ourselves,
the argument that refutes death,
the genius that invents the future,
all we know of God.

It is the serum which makes us swear
not to betray one another;
it is in this poem, trying to speak.

Letter from the End
of the World

The reason no longer matters,
the lamp, my curiosity,
my sisters' insinuations,
never waking up together,
you saying, *trust me.*

The point is the end of innocence
comes when you look at someone you love
asleep and see how his eyeballs flicker
under their shallow lids.

The point is since I lost you
I have been going around the world
looking for you and finding myself
instead, small scraps of a woman
that are beginning to fit.

At first the mountains closed ranks against me,
blackberries dried in my mouth,
the wind kept turning to face me.
Wherever I came, the music stopped,
sidewalks opened up manholes,
lights went out,
a pregnant woman shielded her face.

But I learned to sleep on the ground
despite the heartbeat of giant oaks
and the moon's soft taunts at the sun,
the all-night labor of heaving roots,
the mushroom smell of death.

I learned not to throw the bouquets
the wretched made of their wounds
back in their faces, to accept
tears brought me on red pillows,
to knock on plain white doors
without windows or peepholes, not knowing
whose voice would say, *Come in.*

The point is I came back
from the deep places. Always
there was help, a man or woman
who asked no questions, an animal's
warm body, the itch in my muscles

to climb a swinging rope.

I started out as a girl
without a shadow, in iron shoes;
now, at the end of the world
I am a woman full of rain.
The journey back should be easy;
if this reaches you, wait for me.